BEYOND the BRAIN

UNLOCKING THE HIDDEN POWER OF CONSCIOUSNESS FOR A HAPPIER, HEALTHIER LIFE

J.R. SANTANA

First published 2026

TABLE OF CONTENTS

INTRODUCTION

THE EMPTY CATHEDRAL

Let me tell you a story. In the final days of her life, Margaret didn't recognize her own daughter. Alzheimer's had slowly erased the details of her world—names, faces, even the thread that tied her days together. By the time she entered hospice, it seemed like the person she'd been was already gone. She stared past visitors, spoke in fragments, or not at all. Her doctors explained, gently, that this was what happens. The neurons that held her memories were dying. The Margaret everyone knew was, for all practical purposes, lost.

But then, just two hours before she died, something remarkable happened. Margaret sat up in bed, looked her daughter in the eye, and said, "You've been crying again. Don't worry. I'm all right." She remembered her grandchildren's names. She asked about a family argument from weeks before. She even cracked a joke—dry, a little mischievous, unmistakably hers. For a brief, shining moment, the fog lifted. Margaret was back. And then, just as quickly, she was gone.

This isn't just a touching anecdote. It's a phenomenon with a name: terminal lucidity. For centuries, doctors, nurses, and families have witnessed moments like this—patients with advanced dementia or severe brain injuries suddenly regaining clarity, presence, even humor, right before death. It's not rare. It's just inconvenient for our current scientific models.

Here's the puzzle: If memory is stored in neurons, and those neurons are destroyed, how can someone suddenly remember? It's like smashing a hard drive and watching it briefly boot up to say goodbye. According to the dominant model of the mind, this shouldn't happen. And yet, it does.

Terminal lucidity is just one of many experiences that don't fit neatly into our scientific story. Maybe you've had a moment when you knew who was calling before your phone rang. Or you've walked into a room and felt tension in the air, even though no one was speaking. Maybe you've felt grief as a physical ache in your chest, or had an idea arrive fully formed, as if delivered rather than constructed. These aren't supernatural events. They don't require mysticism or blind faith. But they do ask us to reconsider some of our basic assumptions.

For over a century, neuroscience has been working inside a magnificent cathedral. We've mapped its arches and alcoves, catalogued neurotransmitters, traced electrical currents. We know which regions light up when you recognize a face, feel fear, or remember a melody. We can watch blood flow in real time as you fall in love or solve a puzzle. And yet, as our tools have grown more sophisticated, an uncomfortable truth has emerged: the cathedral is empty. Nowhere have we found the "you" who experiences all this. No neuron or cluster of neurons contains your sense of self. Nowhere is the memory of your mother's perfume, or the sting of embarrassment from something you said ten years ago. We can change circuits and alter behavior, but we haven't found the experiencer.

So, we've landed on a clever workaround: maybe consciousness just "emerges" from the brain, like a trick of complexity. Matter, arranged just so, wakes up and starts wondering about itself. It's a neat idea, but for many people, it's deeply unsatisfying.

Let's try a different metaphor. Imagine an old radio—mahogany case, brass dials, a warm orange glow. Turn the knob, and music fills the room. If you didn't know how radios worked, you might assume the music was inside the box. Smash the tubes, and the music stops. You'd conclude the machine created the music. But you'd be missing the broadcast.

The radio doesn't generate the orchestra. It receives it. Damaging the hardware interrupts the signal, but the music itself doesn't vanish. It's still out there, waiting for another receiver. For much of modern science, we've been smashing radios and assuming we've explained the music.

When speech disappears after a stroke, we say the brain produced speech. When memory degrades in dementia, we say the brain stored memory. When personality shifts after injury, we say the brain generated identity. But what we've really shown is that damaging the receiver disrupts reception. We've proven, beyond doubt, that the brain is necessary for human experience. What we haven't proven—and have quietly assumed—is that it's sufficient.

But what if the brain isn't a generator, but a receiver? Suddenly, a whole range of mysteries—terminal lucidity, anxiety, depression, love, creativity—snap into focus. Maybe anxiety isn't irrational fear, but a bandwidth problem. Maybe depression isn't just a chemical deficit, but signal loss. Maybe love isn't just a metaphorical "connection," but something closer to physics.

This book is about a simple but radical shift: your brain doesn't create consciousness. It receives it.

The journey ahead is not a rejection of science, but an invitation to expand its scope. The receiver model doesn't deny the importance of neurons, synapses, or chemistry. It simply asks: what if these are the means by which we access something larger? What if consciousness is not a trick of complexity, but a signal—one that the brain, in all its intricacy, is exquisitely designed to receive, modulate, and express?

If you're ready, let's step into the empty cathedral and listen for the music that might still be playing.

CHAPTER 1
THE BIOLOGIC ANTENNA

Let's begin with a question that, at first, might sound like science fiction: What if your brain isn't the source of your thoughts, but more like an antenna—tuning in to something larger, something not entirely contained within the boundaries of your skull?

For over a century, the dominant metaphor for the brain has been the supercomputer: a dense network of neurons firing off messages, synapses connecting dots, and every thought or feeling generated by the intricate dance of chemistry and electricity. This model has explained much—how we move, react, and process the world. But it leaves us with a stubborn mystery: why does all this activity feel like something? Why is there an inner movie, a sense of "I am," at the heart of experience?

The Mystery Within

Peer inside a neuron and you'll find a world of complexity. Beyond the familiar image of branching dendrites and axons lies a hidden architecture: microtubules, tiny protein scaffolds that vibrate and oscillate. For decades, these were thought to be mere structural supports, like beams in a cathedral. But recent research hints at something more: microtubules may be capable of supporting quantum effects—those strange, non-local phenomena that defy classical explanation. Some scientists have even speculated that these quantum processes might play a role in consciousness itself. The evidence is preliminary, but the implications are profound: what if the brain's true genius is not computation, but resonance?

The Radio Analogy, Revisited

Imagine an old radio: mahogany case, brass dials, a warm orange glow. Turn the knob, and music fills the room. If you didn't know how radios worked, you might assume the music was inside the box. Smash the tubes, and the music stops. You'd conclude the machine created the music. But you'd be missing the broadcast.

The radio doesn't generate the orchestra. It receives it. Damaging the hardware interrupts the signal, but the music itself doesn't vanish. It's still out there, waiting for another receiver. For much of modern science, we've been smashing radios and assuming we've explained the music.

The Limits of the Generator Model

When speech disappears after a stroke, we say the brain produced speech. When memory degrades in dementia, we say the brain stored memory. When personality shifts after injury, we say the brain generated identity. But what we've really shown is that damaging the receiver disrupts reception. We've proven, beyond doubt, that the brain is necessary for human experience. What we haven't proven—and have quietly assumed—is that it's sufficient.

But what if the brain isn't a generator, but a receiver? Suddenly, a whole range of mysteries—terminal lucidity, anxiety, depression, love, creativity—snap into focus. Maybe anxiety isn't irrational fear, but a bandwidth problem. Maybe depression isn't just a chemical deficit, but signal loss. Maybe love isn't just a metaphorical "connection," but something closer to physics.

The Brain as a Tuner

Let's push the metaphor further. Radios don't create music; they pick up signals that are already out there. If you damage the antenna, the music gets fuzzy or disappears—but the broadcast itself hasn't gone anywhere. In the same way, when parts of the brain are damaged, people might lose the ability to speak, see, or remember, but the sense of being present—the feeling of "I am"—often lingers. Maybe, just maybe, the brain isn't generating consciousness from scratch. Maybe it's picking it up, filtering it, translating it into the experience of being you.

Paradoxes of Consciousness

Here's another twist: Some of the most profound states of consciousness—deep meditation, creative flow, psychedelic experiences—happen when certain parts of the brain actually quiet down. If the brain were a generator, you'd expect less activity to mean less experience. But the opposite seems to be true. When the "self-monitoring" parts of the brain take a break, people often report feeling more connected, more alive, more themselves than ever. So what's going on? Maybe too much brain activity is like static on the radio—too much noise, not enough signal. When the noise drops, the signal comes through loud and clear.

The Brain's True Genius

Of course, this doesn't mean the brain isn't important. Far from it. If the brain is an antenna, it's a highly sophisticated one, evolved over millions of years to tune in just enough to help us survive. Too much signal, and we'd be overwhelmed. Too little, and we'd be lost. The brain's genius might not be in creating consciousness, but in filtering it—letting in just enough to make life possible.

And that's where things get really fascinating. If the brain is a receiver, then understanding how it tunes in, filters, and sometimes distorts the signal of consciousness could change everything about how we think about ourselves, our minds, and even our place in the universe.

A New Orientation

This chapter is not a rejection of neuroscience, but an invitation to expand its scope. The receiver model doesn't deny the importance of neurons, synapses, or chemistry. It simply asks: what if these are the means by which we access something larger? What if consciousness is not a trick of complexity, but a signal—one that the brain, in all its intricacy, is exquisitely designed to receive, modulate, and express?

Ready to see where this signal leads? Let's keep going.

CHAPTER 2
THE FILTER

Let's be honest: if you truly noticed everything happening around you, you'd never get anything done. Imagine standing at a busy intersection, every detail clamoring for your attention—the glint of sunlight on a windshield, the rhythm of footsteps, the distant hum of a siren, the subtle shift in the air as a bus passes. If your mind absorbed it all, you'd be paralyzed by the sheer volume of sensation. The world is not just rich; it's overwhelming. Survival demands selectivity.

The Reducing Valve

Back in the 1950s, Aldous Huxley called the brain a "reducing valve." He meant that reality is bursting with more information than any of us could possibly handle, and our brains are designed to narrow it down to just what's useful. At the time, people thought he was being poetic. Now, it sounds a lot like engineering. The filter is not a flaw—it's a feature. It's the reason you can focus on a conversation in a noisy café, or ignore the ticking of a clock until someone points it out.

Every sense you have—sight, hearing, touch—comes with its own built-in editing system. Your eyes fill in blind spots. Your ears tune out constant background noise. Even your sense of touch fades into the background unless something changes. And your consciousness? It's doing the same thing, all the time. The filter isn't asking, "What's true?" It's asking, "What's useful right now?"

Evolution's Tunnel

Evolution doesn't reward accuracy. It rewards survival. Our ancestors didn't make it because they saw the world perfectly. They made it because they saw what they needed to see to stay alive. That's why the world feels stable, even though it's not. Objects seem solid, even though they're mostly empty space. Time feels like it moves in a straight line, even though physics says otherwise. Your filter enforces these illusions because they help you function.

Think of your attention like a tunnel. You experience the world through a narrow beam, built from your senses, your emotions, and what you've learned matters. Everything outside that tunnel gets filtered out—not because it's unreal, but because it's not useful. The mistake we make is assuming the tunnel is reality. Science sometimes insists only the tunnel exists; spirituality sometimes tries to escape it entirely. Both miss the point.

The Ego as Firewall

Psychologists talk about the ego as the part of you that plans, judges, and worries. But in this model, the ego is more like a firewall. It doesn't create your thoughts—it decides which ones get through. It's constantly filtering your experience, keeping out anything that might destabilize your sense of self. It's so good at this job that we often mistake its version of reality for the real thing.

Neuroscientists have a name for the brain's main filter: the Default Mode Network, or DMN. This network lights up when you're thinking about yourself—replaying memories, rehearsing your story, worrying about the future. When the DMN is active, your experience narrows. But when it quiets down, something amazing happens. The sense of self softens.

Time gets weird. Sights and sounds become more vivid. People report feeling more connected, more present, more alive. This happens in meditation, creative flow, deep focus, and even psychedelic states. Less ego, more experience.

Loosening the Filter

So, what happens when the filter loosens? When resistance drops—temporarily and safely—your experience expands. You get bursts of creativity, flashes of insight, deeper emotional processing. You see beyond your usual constraints, but you don't lose your grip on reality. The key is that the filter loosens, but doesn't disappear.

But if the filter fails completely, it's not enlightenment—it's overload. Everything feels important. Patterns pop up everywhere. Meaning multiplies without order. This isn't clarity; it's chaos. Psychotic states are what happen when the filter breaks down entirely. Information floods in without context or ownership. The mind can't prioritize, and it drowns in significance. The filter exists for a reason.

Childhood and Culture

Children are a natural experiment in filtering. Young kids have wild imaginations, intense emotions, and experiences that seem uncanny to adults. As they grow, these fade—not because they're learning reality, but because their filters are hardening. The ego consolidates, resistance increases, and they become better at functioning, but worse at perceiving beyond the tunnel. It's a necessary trade-off.

Culture adds another layer of filtering. Language, norms, and beliefs train your attention toward some things and away from others. Modern life introduces a new problem: constant partial openness. Notifications, media, and social comparison keep your receiver in a state of perpetual alert. The filter never fully closes, and the system never rests. The result isn't awareness—it's exhaustion.

Adjustability: The Sweet Spot

The goal isn't to remove the filter, but to adjust it. A healthy receiver can narrow bandwidth for focus and survival, then widen it for creativity, connection, and insight. Too much rigidity leads to numbness; too much openness leads to chaos. The sweet spot is adjustability.

Understanding your filter changes how you think about mental health, attention, and even morality. Being overwhelmed isn't weakness. Numbness isn't failure. Intrusive thoughts aren't your identity. They're regulation problems—and regulation can be learned.

Beyond the Filter: Memory as Access

Next, let's look at what happens to information once it gets through the filter. Where does it go? How does it come back? And why do some memories resurface decades later? To answer that, we need to rethink memory—not as storage, but as access.

CHAPTER 3

THE CLOUD (MEMORY)

Let's talk about memory. Most of us imagine our brains as a kind of high-tech filing cabinet. You have an experience, you "store" it somewhere in your head, and when you need it, you pull it out, dust it off, and relive it. Simple, right? But the reality is far stranger, and far more wondrous.

The Search for the Engram

For decades, scientists searched for the "engram"—the physical trace of a memory in the brain. The idea was straightforward: if memories are stored in specific spots, then removing the right bit of brain tissue should erase the corresponding memory. But when researchers tried this with rats, they found something surprising. No matter which part of the brain they removed, the rats still remembered how to run a maze. They might get slower or clumsier, but the knowledge itself stuck around. It was as if memory was everywhere and nowhere at once.

This finding didn't just puzzle scientists—it upended the very metaphor we use for memory. If memories aren't stored like files in a cabinet, what's really going on?

Memory as Tuning, Not Storage

Here's a different way to think about it: Your brain doesn't store memories—it streams them. When you remember your childhood home, you're not opening a file hidden in your neurons. You're tuning in to a pattern, like finding the right frequency on a radio. The brain isn't the archive; it's the interface.

This explains a lot of the weirdness around memory. For example, people with advanced dementia sometimes have moments of sudden clarity right before death—remembering names, faces, and stories that seemed long gone. If memories were just stored in brain tissue, this shouldn't be possible. But if the brain is a receiver, maybe what's really happening is that, as the body shuts down, the filter loosens, resistance drops, and the signal comes through one last time.

Memory as Coordinates in Spacetime

Think of memory as a set of coordinates. Every experience you have happens at a specific point in space and time. When you remember, you're not reconstructing the past from scratch—you're tuning back into that moment. That's why some memories feel so vivid, like you're reliving them, not just recalling them.

But memory isn't perfect. It's shaped by the state you're in. You remember different things when you're calm than when you're stressed, or when you're alone versus with others. Sometimes, memories pop up when you least expect them—during a walk, in the shower, or right before sleep. That's not a bug; it's a feature of how your receiver works.

Music and Memory

Music is a great example. People who can't remember their own children's names can often sing entire songs from their youth, word for word. Music acts like a tuning fork, helping the brain lock onto a familiar pattern and restore access, even when other channels are blocked.

Trauma and the Firewall

And what about trauma? Traumatic memories aren't just stored incorrectly—they're stored too well. Flashbacks aren't just recollections; they're re-experiences. The past crashes into the present, full force. The receiver has lost its ability to filter, and the memory floods in without warning.

Forgetting, then, isn't failure—it's temporary disconnection. The memory isn't gone; you just can't access it right now. Healing from trauma isn't about erasing memories, but about restoring safe, controlled access.

The Cloud Connection

So, what does all this mean? If memory is about access, not storage, then aging, trauma, and even everyday forgetfulness look different. Nothing meaningful is wasted. Every moment you've lived is woven into the fabric of your experience, shaping who you are—even if you can't always call it up on demand.

In the end, your brain isn't a vault. It's a cloud connection. Sometimes the signal is strong, sometimes it's weak, but the archive is always there, waiting for you to tune in.

Looking Ahead

Next up: What happens when the signal gets noisy? Let's look at anxiety, depression, and the static that can make life feel overwhelming.

CHAPTER 4
SIGNAL NOISE (ANXIETY & DEPRESSION)

Let's talk about something almost everyone deals with at some point: anxiety and depression. If you've ever been told your mind is "malfunctioning," you're not alone. The usual explanation is chemical—too much of this, not enough of that, a circuit misfiring somewhere in your brain. It's a tidy story, and it's partly true. But if you ask people what anxiety or depression actually feels like, you'll get a very different answer.

People with anxiety rarely say, "I feel chemically imbalanced." Instead, they talk about feeling flooded—racing thoughts, a body braced for impact, a future that feels immediate and unavoidable. Depression isn't just sadness. It's absence, flatness, disconnection—a silence where color and motivation used to live. These aren't just poetic descriptions; they're clues to what's really going on.

Signal Regulation: A New Lens

Here's a new way to look at it: anxiety and depression aren't failures of mood or character. They're failures of signal regulation. Imagine your brain as a receiver, picking up signals from the world around you. Sometimes, the receiver gets overloaded—too much information, too many possible futures, all at once. That's anxiety. Other times, the signal drops out, and everything feels muted and gray. That's depression.

Anxiety: When the Future Leaks In

Anxiety is often described as fear without cause, but it doesn't feel imaginary. It feels very real, very present. Your body reacts as if something is happening right now—muscles tense, heart races, breathing shortens. Under the receiver model, anxiety is "signal bleed." Your filter isn't working as it should, and possible futures start to intrude. The body doesn't distinguish between potential and actual threat, so it reacts to both.

Ever get stuck in "what if" mode? What if I fail? What if something goes wrong? What if I missed something important? These aren't random worries—they're partial downloads. Your mind is sampling too many timelines at once, each demanding attention. The result? Paralysis. Panic attacks are the extreme version: the receiver is flooded, and the fight-or-flight response kicks in even when there's no immediate danger.

Some people are especially sensitive to signal. They pick up on emotional shifts quickly, feel overwhelmed by crowds or unpredictability, and anticipate problems before anyone else. These "high-gain receivers" are great at empathy and intuition, but they're also prone to chronic overload. Modern life—with its constant stimulation and social comparison—isn't designed for sensitive receivers. It's like running a precision instrument without any shielding.

Depression: When the Signal Drops Out

If anxiety is excess signal, depression is signal loss. It's not just a feeling—it's the absence of feeling. The world flattens, motivation evaporates, meaning thins. Depression is like interference—the antenna is intact, but access to the signal weakens. That's why depression is exhausting, why even simple tasks feel insurmountable, and why clarity sometimes returns for no apparent reason. The connection breaks through one day, and then it doesn't the next.

Anxiety and depression often cycle together. Chronic signal bleed produces anxiety. The system strains to process excess data, then shuts down to prevent damage. Depression, in this context, isn't the opposite of anxiety—it's a circuit breaker. The mind isn't weak; it's protecting itself.

Chemistry Revisited

None of this denies the role of neurochemistry. Chemicals regulate resistance and influence bandwidth. Medication can be lifesaving because it stabilizes tuning. But chemistry is the knob, not the broadcast. Treating anxiety and depression solely as chemical problems is like adjusting the volume without asking what's playing.

Environmental Noise

Mental health doesn't happen in isolation. Modern life bombards us with low-grade threat—news cycles, notifications, social metrics, artificial urgency. Our nervous systems evolved for intermittent danger and long periods of quiet, but now we get constant stimulation with no recovery. It's not resilience—it's erosion.

Relational Interference

Other people are among the strongest signals we encounter. Chronic conflict, unpredictability, and invalidation act as persistent interference. That's why anxiety often decreases when people leave toxic environments—before any internal work begins, the signal clears. Supportive relationships stabilize tuning, reduce noise, and allow the filter to relax safely. Mental health isn't just internal; it's relational physics.

Signal Hygiene

If anxiety and depression are signal problems, then healing involves signal hygiene. That means protecting attention from constant interruption, creating genuine silence, regulating exposure to threat-based media, establishing predictable rhythms of sleep and movement, and limiting destabilizing relationships. Without these, deeper interventions struggle to take hold.

Meaning and Noise

One of the worst effects of anxiety and depression is the loss of meaning. Life feels arbitrary, and effort feels pointless. Under the receiver model, meaning isn't imposed—it's detected. When the signal clears, meaning reappears. When noise dominates, meaning collapses. Restoring signal integrity is crucial for restoring the capacity for meaning.

Therapy as Retuning

At its best, therapy isn't about fixing broken thoughts—it's about retuning. A stable, attuned relationship reduces noise. Insight alone rarely heals, but regulation does. That's why the relationship between therapist and client matters more than technique.

Identity and Noise

Long-term anxiety or depression often fuses with identity. People become "anxious" or "depressed" rather than people experiencing interference. This hardens resistance and complicates change. Under the receiver model, identity remains separate from signal quality. You are not your noise; you are the system experiencing it.

The Next Distortion

Anxiety and depression involve excess and absence, but there's another disturbance: what happens when signal arrives without ownership? When information intrudes without context or control? To understand this, we need to look at "the glitch"—psychosis and hallucination.

CHAPTER 5
THE GLITCH (SCHIZOPHRENIA & HALLUCINATION)

Let's talk about something that makes most people uncomfortable: experiences that don't fit inside the usual frame of reality. Hallucinations, voices, delusions—these are the kinds of things we rush to label as "psychotic" and try to contain as quickly as possible. That urgency is understandable. But in our rush to manage, we often miss the chance to understand.

Signal Without Ownership

Here's what's fascinating: when you ask someone who hears voices what it feels like, they don't say, "I'm making this up." They say, "It arrives." The voice intrudes, insists, and feels real—sometimes even more real than their own thoughts. In the receiver model, this distinction matters. Psychosis isn't about inventing false content; it's about signal arriving without ownership.

A healthy receiver does two things at once: it samples information, and it tags that information as "mine" or "not mine." Most of us don't question whether our inner voice is ours, or whether imagination is different from perception. The filter assigns provenance automatically. But in psychosis, this process breaks down. Thoughts arrive, but the "ownership tag" is missing. Inner speech becomes an external voice. Meaning floods in, but there's no hierarchy. The glitch isn't that something unreal appears—it's that context fails to attach.

The Intensity of Psychosis

One of the most misunderstood aspects of psychosis is its intensity. Hallucinations aren't usually random; they feel urgent, personal, even revelatory. Clinicians sometimes dismiss them as symbolic expressions of subconscious conflict. Sometimes they are, but often they're more literal. In the receiver model, psychosis is a collapse of salience filtering. Everything feels significant because nothing is dampened. The result? Conviction without clarity—a system that can't tell signal from noise.

Dopamine and the Importance Knob

Dopamine plays a starring role here. Antipsychotic medications reduce dopamine signaling and often reduce hallucinations. This has led to the idea that dopamine causes psychosis. But the receiver model offers a different take: dopamine is the "importance knob." When it's out of whack, everything gets flagged as important. Medication turns down the volume, restoring resistance, but it can also flatten emotional experience. The signal is quieter, but sometimes life feels duller, too.

Culture as a Buffer

Culture matters more than we think. In societies where hallucinations are interpreted as spiritual experiences, people with psychotic traits often fare better. Voices are contextualized, ritualized, and contained. In Western cultures, voices are medicalized, feared, and fought. The difference isn't belief—it's environmental buffering. A receiver overwhelmed by signal does worse in a hostile environment than in a supportive one. This doesn't romanticize psychosis, but it does put it in context.

It's tempting to see psychosis as expanded consciousness gone wrong, but that's dangerous. Psychosis isn't insight—it's exposure without insulation. True insight integrates; psychosis fragments. True clarity stabilizes; psychosis destabilizes. The receiver model doesn't elevate psychosis, but it does explain why it hurts.

Distinguishing Insight from Psychosis

So how do we tell the difference between insight and psychosis? Insight can be reflected upon, tolerates doubt, integrates with reality, and doesn't demand immediate action. Psychosis feels urgent, resists questioning, overrides context, and demands a response. The difference matters. Psychosis is signal flooding without integration. The channel is open, but the system can't metabolize what arrives. This isn't expansion—it's exposure.

Culture acts as a secondary filter. Where hallucinations are contextualized and bounded, people often experience less distress and better outcomes. Where they're framed only as pathology, fear and isolation dominate. The receiver model says: culture provides containment. Where this is absent, the individual bears the full burden alone.

Medication, Structure, and Containment

Medication is often necessary, but it's not a cure-all. It increases resistance, restoring boundaries and reducing flooding. But medication alone isn't enough. Psychosis is relational and environmental, too. Noise, unpredictability, trauma, sleep deprivation, and isolation all degrade boundaries. A stabilized receiver placed back into a destabilizing environment will relapse. Containment is not just pharmacological—it's ecological.

Structure—routines, predictable environments, even hospital stays—aren't punishment. They're external regulation while internal regulation recovers. Freedom without regulation isn't freedom; it's exposure.

Validation and Limits

There's a trend toward validating all subjective experience. Validation is essential, but without limits, it becomes abdication. The receiver model allows validation without endorsement: "Your experience is real. Your suffering is real. But not every signal deserves obedience." That distinction can be life-saving.

Trauma, Vulnerability, and Early Intervention

Psychosis often emerges at the intersection of vulnerability and stress. Trauma destabilizes boundaries, identity fractures, and the receiver becomes permeable. The signal arrives without containment. Themes of persecution, guilt, control, and revelation aren't random—they reflect unresolved emotional signal amplified without filter. Addressing trauma means restoring safety and regulation first.

Early intervention matters. The longer psychosis persists, the harder it is to treat—not because beliefs become entrenched, but because the receiver adapts to chaos. Early intervention restores boundaries before adaptation solidifies.

Creativity, Permeability, and Responsibility

Many people with psychotic vulnerabilities are also highly creative. Permeability increases access to novel associations. Healthy creatives learn when to open and when to close. Psychosis removes that choice. Romanticizing psychosis ignores this and puts vulnerable people at risk.

The receiver model removes moral blame from psychosis, but not responsibility. People experiencing psychosis aren't at fault, but they are responsible for managing it with support. Care systems aren't obligated to validate every belief—they're obligated to reduce suffering and protect life.

The Necessity of Constraint

Psychosis challenges our cultural myths. It shows that meaning can overwhelm, that insight can injure, and that openness without boundary is not liberation. It also exposes a deeper truth: the mind's filters exist because life requires constraint. Remove constraint entirely, and you don't awaken—you disappear.

So, psychosis isn't evidence against the receiver model. It's evidence of what happens when reception loses governance. The signal may be real, but the access isn't survivable. Understanding this lets us respond with clarity, care, and prepares us for the next question: If unregulated openness destroys coherence, and rigid closure destroys meaning, where's the balance? The answer lies not in pathology, but in attachment.

CHAPTER 6
THE NETWORK (CROWDS & VIBES)

Let's shift gears and talk about something you've probably felt, even if you've never put words to it: the energy of a crowd. Ever walked into a room and instantly sensed tension, even though nobody said a word? Or felt the electric excitement in a stadium just before the big game? Maybe you've noticed how moods seem to ripple through a group, or how a "vibe" can change everything. These moments aren't just poetic—they're real, and they're part of how our minds connect.

Resonance Beyond Words

For a long time, we've been taught to think of our minds as private, sealed off from everyone else. Communication, we're told, happens through words, gestures, deliberate signals sent from one person to another. But that's only part of the story. Human nervous systems are incredibly sensitive to each other. Long before language, our bodies were communicating—through posture, facial expressions, breathing, and movement. This isn't just metaphor; it's called entrainment.

In physics, entrainment is when oscillating systems sync up. Pendulum clocks on the same wall eventually swing together. Fireflies flash in unison. Even heart cells in a dish coordinate their rhythms. Humans do this too. Our heart rates, breathing patterns, and emotional states can synchronize with those around us. Under the receiver model, this isn't just mimicry—it's network resonance. When we're tuned to similar frequencies and close together, we start to share a signal.

The Heart's Broadcast

And it's not just the brain. The heart generates an electromagnetic field that can be measured several feet beyond your skin. Research suggests this field carries information about your emotional state. Calm, coherent heart rhythms correlate with clarity; chaotic rhythms with stress. When people interact, these fields overlap. No mysticism required—just biophysics. Some people seem to calm a room just by walking in; others raise tension without saying a word. They're not "giving off vibes"—they're broadcasting coherence, or noise.

Crowd Dynamics

Crowds are fascinating. Sometimes, a group of people behaves less like individuals and more like a single organism. Mobs escalate faster than anyone intends. Audiences experience shared euphoria. Religious gatherings can produce collective trance. These effects happen too quickly to be explained by conscious imitation. Under the receiver model, crowds are temporary super-receivers. As individual filters loosen—through music, danger, ritual, or anonymity—the network synchronizes. Emotional signal circulates freely, identity blurs, and responsibility diffuses. This can be ecstatic, but it can also be catastrophic.

Rational thought is slow, but emotional contagion is instant. That's why crowds can turn volatile without leadership, why markets panic, why outrage spreads faster than correction. Once emotional resonance hits a critical threshold, information bypasses individual filters. People don't decide to feel—they catch feeling. It's not weakness; it's architecture.

Urban Overload

Cities are a special case. Urban environments concentrate receivers—millions of nervous systems operating at high gain, generating persistent background noise. Vigilance, urgency, and stress saturate the field. People living in cities often report exhaustion unrelated to workload. The body never fully powers down; the receiver never fully closes. Under the receiver model, this is network overload. Solitude becomes restorative not because of introspection, but because it breaks resonance.

Technology and the Global Nervous System

Technology takes this even further. Social platforms synchronize emotional states among millions who will never meet. Fear spikes globally. Outrage cascades. Hope surges and collapses. These platforms amplify high-salience signals because those propagate fastest. Calm doesn't go viral, but anger does. The result? A global nervous system stuck in partial fight-or-flight. Never before have human receivers synchronized at this scale without shared ritual, containment, or recovery.

Ever feel drained after social interaction—even positive interaction? That's not just introversion; it's signal fatigue. Maintaining coherence within a network takes energy. Your receiver is constantly adjusting to others' emotional states. After prolonged exposure, recalibration is required. Solitude isn't avoidance—it's maintenance.

Networks in Families and Workplaces

Network effects operate powerfully in small systems too. Families develop emotional fields. Children entrain to caregivers long before language. Calm stabilizes; anxiety teaches vigilance. The same goes for workplaces. You can often sense an office's emotional climate within minutes. Productivity flows or stalls, conversations tighten or relax. This atmosphere rarely comes from one person—it emerges from shared stressors, incentives, and unspoken norms. Toxic environments harm not through overt cruelty, but through ambient distortion.

Leadership, at its core, is signal management. Effective leaders regulate emotional fields. They dampen panic, clarify priorities, and prevent runaway amplification of threat. Poor leaders inject volatility, escalate emotion, and destabilize filters. Leadership is less about charisma than about coherence.

Ritual, Connection, and Withdrawal

Traditional societies understood network regulation intuitively. Rituals—religious, seasonal, communal—synchronized emotion deliberately. They provided rhythm, allowing collective release without collapse. Modern societies have largely abandoned ritual while retaining constant connectivity. The result? A network with no reset mechanism, where emotion accumulates without resolution.

Not all networks are healthy. Some amplify fear, reward outrage, or trap individuals in comparison and inadequacy. Leaving such networks isn't weakness—it's recalibration. The receiver can't retune while submerged in static.

But complete withdrawal carries its own cost. Human receivers evolved for connection. Prolonged isolation weakens regulation. Depression and anxiety rise when network input drops below a critical threshold. The goal isn't immersion or isolation, but a balance of selective connection.

Responsibility in the Network

If emotion propagates, responsibility expands. You're not responsible for others' feelings, but you are responsible for what you amplify. Tone, attention, and emotional posture all contribute to shared signal. Chronic cynicism and outrage aren't private states—they're broadcasts. This isn't emotional policing; it's physics.

So, the receiver model expands from individual minds to shared systems. But one question remains: If receivers synchronize automatically, is agency possible? Can we tune deliberately, rather than reactively? To answer that, we need to look at moments when the channel clears voluntarily—when insight flows, creativity emerges, and action feels effortless. Let's learn how receivers tune in.

CHAPTER 7
TUNING IN (INTUITION & CREATIVITY)

Let's talk about those moments when your best ideas seem to come out of nowhere. You know the feeling: you're stuck on a problem, you try to force a solution, and nothing happens. Then, when you're walking the dog, taking a shower, or staring out the window, the answer just pops into your head. We have all sorts of casual ways to describe this: "It came to me," "I had a download," "It just appeared." These aren't just figures of speech—they're actually pretty accurate descriptions of how creativity and intuition work.

The Air of Discovery

Throughout history, big discoveries have often happened in parallel. Calculus was developed independently by Newton and Leibniz. Darwin and Wallace both came up with evolution by natural selection. Oxygen was identified by several scientists at almost the same time. It's as if these ideas were "in the air," waiting for someone to tune in. Maybe creativity isn't about inventing something from nothing, but about detecting what's ready to be found.

What Is Intuition?

So, what is intuition? It's often dismissed as guesswork, but in reality, intuition is your brain's way of rapidly integrating patterns—synthesizing sensory, emotional, and contextual information before you can even explain it. The result arrives as a gut feeling: "This is right," or "This is wrong." Intuition doesn't feel vague; what feels vague is our ability to justify it. Rational thought is slow and step-by-step. Intuition is fast and all-at-once.

The Flow State

Then there's flow—the state where everything just clicks. Athletes, musicians, writers, and even surgeons describe flow in similar ways: effortlessness, time distortion, loss of self-consciousness, and peak performance. Neuroscience shows that during flow, the self-monitoring parts of the brain quiet down. The filter relaxes, but doesn't collapse. Under the receiver model, flow is optimal tuning: the antenna is clear, resistance is calibrated, and the signal moves through without obstruction. You're not forcing performance—you're allowing it.

This explains a familiar paradox: the harder you try to force insight, the less likely it is to arrive. Effort increases resistance, the ego tightens its grip, and the receiver clamps down. That's why solutions often appear when you stop looking. Relaxation lowers resistance. Play widens the channel. Even boredom—real, undistracted boredom—creates receptivity.

The Liminal Mind

Many people notice they're especially clear-headed right after waking up. That's no accident. During sleep, the ego relaxes, memory integrates, and emotional noise settles. In those liminal moments before your inner narrator kicks in, resistance is low and coherence is high. Ideas arrive because the channel is open. That's why keeping a notebook by your bed works so well.

Authorship and Translation

But if ideas are received, why do they feel so personal? Because the decoding is personal. The signal might be shared, but your translation is unique—shaped by your skills, history, and perspective. Two people can receive the same idea and express it in completely different ways. Authorship lies in the expression, not the origin. This doesn't diminish creativity—it grounds it.

Tuning Is Procedural

Tuning isn't mystical; it's procedural. Creative traditions across cultures converge on similar practices: silence, repetition, ritual, constraint, movement, and deliberate rest. These aren't just aesthetic choices—they're ways to condition the signal. Ritual reduces uncertainty, constraint limits noise, repetition trains attention, and movement regulates the body. The receiver isn't persuaded; it's trained.

Frustration is feedback. When effort meets resistance, the system overheats. Stepping away isn't failure—it's retuning.

Bandwidth and Maintenance

Of course, bandwidth matters. Fatigue, stress, and emotional overload degrade reception. Creativity doesn't disappear because talent vanishes, but because the system is saturated. Rest isn't indulgence—it's essential maintenance.

Intuition vs. Delusion

Not every signal should be trusted. The difference between intuition and delusion isn't content—it's constraint. Intuition arrives quietly, tolerates scrutiny, and integrates with reality. Delusion arrives loudly, resists testing, and demands immediate action. A healthy receiver samples signals without surrendering to them.

Time is a reliable filter. True insights age well—they remain coherent after sleep, conversation, and challenge. False signals decay; their urgency fades. That's why disciplined creatives develop habits of postponement: they write ideas down, return later, and test gently. Humility is a tuning mechanism.

Expanded access can tempt ego inflation. When ideas arrive with clarity, it's easy to identify with them. But if ideas are accessed rather than authored, the right posture is stewardship, not possession. Gratitude replaces entitlement; discipline replaces myth. Many great creators describe themselves as conduits—not out of modesty, but precision.

Everyday Tuning

Tuning isn't just for artists. Everyday decisions—choosing relationships, sensing misalignment, knowing when to leave—often rely on subtle cues that resist explanation. The receiver synthesizes information faster than conscious thought. Ignoring intuition entirely is as risky as trusting it blindly.

Insight carries responsibility. Ideas shape behavior, creativity influences culture, and intuition guides action. But a receiver tuned without ethical grounding can amplify harm as easily as beauty. That's why enduring traditions pair inspiration with discipline, humility, and service. The signal may be neutral, but its use is not.

The Journey Continues

So far, we've traced consciousness from antenna to filter, from noise to network, from tuning to insight. What remains is the most emotionally charged phenomenon of all: attachment. Why does love feel like connection rather than choice? Why does grief feel like tearing rather than sadness? Why does loss echo long after separation? To answer these, we need to look at tethers—the resonant bonds that form between minds.

CHAPTER 8
THE TETHER (LOVE & GRIEF)

Let's talk about love—the one experience that refuses to fit neatly into any box. Science tries to explain it with chemicals like oxytocin and dopamine, or with psychological theories about attachment and projection. Society wraps it up in contracts, expectations, and cultural scripts. All of these explanations help, but none quite capture why love feels like connection, not just preference. Or why losing someone feels less like sadness and more like something being torn away.

Resonance and Attachment

When two people interact deeply and repeatedly, something subtle but measurable happens. Their emotional rhythms start to align. Their nervous systems anticipate each other. Presence becomes regulatory; absence becomes destabilizing. This isn't just poetry—it's resonance. In physics, resonant systems exchange energy efficiently. Once coupled, changes in one system affect the other. Human attachment works the same way. Love isn't just liking someone intensely—it's frequency locking.

People rarely describe falling in love as a decision. They say it "just happened," or "clicked," or "felt familiar." Under the receiver model, love begins when two systems recognize compatibility below conscious analysis. The match is detected through resonance, not reasoning. That's why love can bypass logic and override caution. The receiver has tuned.

Regulation and Tethering

Attachment research shows that bonded individuals regulate each other's physiology. Stress hormones drop in the presence of an attachment figure. Pain tolerance increases. Heart rhythms synchronize. These effects persist even in absence. Once resonance is established, physical proximity isn't required for influence. The tether remains active. That's why you can sense someone's mood from afar, why distance strains bonds without erasing them, and why separation hurts even when you're still in touch digitally.

Deep relationships expand capacity. People in secure attachments report increased resilience, creativity, and emotional range. Not because love fixes them, but because shared resonance stabilizes tuning. Two receivers sharing the load reduce noise. They act as mutual insulation against a volatile field. Love isn't a luxury—it's infrastructure.

But resonance doesn't guarantee health. Sometimes, we bond with people who reproduce familiar emotional frequencies, even when those frequencies are painful. The receiver doesn't ask, "Is this good for me?" It asks, "Is this known?" That's why destructive relationships can feel so compelling. Breaking those bonds requires more than insight—it requires retuning.

The Physiology of Loss

Attachment is felt physically. Love warms the chest, grief constricts the throat, and loss produces real pain. Under the receiver model, this is literal. The body is part of the antenna. When a tether forms, regulation becomes shared. When it breaks, the system scrambles to compensate. Grief isn't just sadness—it's signal withdrawal.

Grief rarely fades smoothly. It comes in waves—overwhelming, then absent, then suddenly present again. Triggers appear without warning. Under the receiver model, this reflects intermittent reconnection. The tether doesn't vanish at separation or death; it destabilizes, and the system repeatedly tries to re-establish access. Each attempt fails, and each failure hurts. Over time, the receiver learns not that the bond was unreal, but that it's no longer available in the same way.

Attachment Styles as Tuning Patterns

Attachment theory is often presented clinically, stripped of texture and consequence. We talk about secure, anxious, and avoidant attachment styles as if they're personality traits. But under the receiver model, attachment styles are tuning patterns—learned ways of regulating resonance with others. They're not choices; they're adaptations.

The first relationships in a human life do more than teach behavior—they calibrate the receiver. Infants arrive with open channels and minimal filtration. Caregivers regulate arousal, threat, and comfort externally. Over time, these patterns are internalized. A predictable caregiver teaches the nervous system that connection stabilizes. An inconsistent caregiver teaches vigilance. An unavailable caregiver teaches self-reliance at the cost of resonance. These lessons aren't remembered—they're embedded. The receiver learns what level of openness is survivable.

Secure attachment isn't constant closeness—it's reliable access. Securely attached people tolerate distance because resonance doesn't collapse in absence. The tether stretches without snapping. The system trusts reconnection. This trust isn't optimism—it's learned physics.

Anxiously attached people experience heightened sensitivity to relational signal. Small changes in tone feel urgent, delays feel threatening, absence feels catastrophic. This is often misinterpreted as neediness, but under the receiver model, it's signal amplification. Early unpredictability taught the system that access can vanish suddenly. The receiver compensates by monitoring constantly, amplifying signal to prevent loss. It's exhausting, but understandable.

Avoidantly attached people suppress resonance. They down-regulate emotional access, minimize dependency, and prioritize autonomy. They often appear composed under stress, which is mistaken for strength. Under the receiver model, it's signal suppression. Early experiences taught the system that openness is costly. The receiver reduces bandwidth to maintain stability. Safety is preserved, but depth is sacrificed.

Attachment styles aren't just habits—they're regulatory patterns operating below conscious choice. Insight alone rarely changes them, but safety does. Retuning requires repeated experiences of stability that contradict early calibration. This takes time.

Love's Disruption and Grief's Recalibration

Love is disruptive because it reactivates early tuning patterns. It destabilizes because it reopens channels that have been carefully regulated. Old adaptations resurface, anxieties intensify, defenses activate. This isn't immaturity—it's signal depth. Love matters because it alters regulation.

Breakups hurt more than logic allows because what actually breaks is shared regulation. Two receivers that had synchronized must suddenly operate independently. Baseline emotional states destabilize. Sleep disrupts, appetite changes, focus collapses. These aren't dramatic reactions—they're withdrawal symptoms.

Grief is recalibration. The system repeatedly tries to access a tether that no longer responds. Each attempt fails, and each failure hurts. Over time, the receiver updates its expectations. The bond wasn't unreal—it just exists in a different form. That's why grief lessens without disappearing. It's the tether transforming.

Modern culture urges "closure," but that's a myth. There's no final severing moment where a meaningful bond disappears. The receiver doesn't delete resonance—it integrates it. Grief resolves not through forgetting, but through reorganization. The bond moves from active regulation to background coherence.

Healthy grief often includes a sense of ongoing connection—internalized presence, guidance, or comfort. This isn't denial; it's integration. Under the receiver model, it's stable resonance without active access. The pattern remains, but the regulation changes.

Grief becomes complicated when recalibration fails. The receiver remains locked in active search mode, the tether can't transform, and the pain persists. This often happens when the loss was sudden or traumatic, the relationship was ambivalent, or there was no opportunity for meaning-making. Treatment focuses not on "letting go," but on restoring regulation. Safety precedes insight.

Continuity, Depth, and the Physics of Bonds

Forming new attachments after loss often triggers guilt. But love isn't a finite resource, and resonance doesn't cancel previous bonds. New tethers don't overwrite old ones—they coexist. Each bond operates at a different frequency and depth.

This understanding allows continuity without betrayal.

From a purely hedonic perspective, love is irrational. It guarantees vulnerability, invites loss, and destabilizes regulation. Yet we seek it, again and again. Under the receiver model, the reason is clear: love expands bandwidth, stabilizes networks, and deepens meaning. The cost is real, but the return is greater.

Grief isn't just the price of love—it's evidence of it. You don't grieve what never regulated you. The intensity of grief matches the depth of resonance. Mourning isn't weakness—it's testament.

As people age, they accumulate tethers. Some are lost, some endure, some transform into memory and meaning. This shapes tuning. Older individuals often experience deeper emotional range and greater vulnerability. The receiver carries more history. This isn't decline—it's density.

Understanding attachment as resonance, not dependency, shifts how we approach relationships. It encourages patience, compassion, respect for distance, and honesty about capacity. It discourages shaming vulnerability, forcing closure, romanticizing suffering, and pathologizing grief.

Breakups and bereavement often require distance—not as punishment, but as signal recalibration. Continued exposure keeps the tether active, but partial access prevents retuning. That's why "staying friends immediately" often prolongs suffering. Distance isn't cruelty—it's repair.

Modern culture treats grief as something to overcome. Prolonged grief is framed as dysfunction or delay. But under the receiver model, grief is relearning. The system updates expectations slowly because the bond mattered deeply. There's no shortcut. Pathologizing grief adds resistance to a process that needs allowance.

Many grieving people report a quiet consolation—a sense that the bond hasn't disappeared entirely. Under the receiver model, this is residual resonance. Once systems synchronize, the pattern doesn't vanish instantly when access ends. The receiver continues to detect traces until retuning completes. This doesn't require belief in literal presence, but it does require persistence of pattern.

Physics offers a careful analogy: quantum entanglement describes systems that remain correlated after separation, not through communication, but through shared state. Human relationships aren't quantum systems, but the analogy clarifies why bonds persist beyond proximity and why separation doesn't immediately erase influence.

Some attachments permanently alter tuning and recalibrate baseline frequencies. They reshape identity and leave signatures that persist. Healing doesn't erase these bonds—it integrates them. Love becomes background coherence, not foreground need.

Forming new bonds after loss can feel like betrayal. But new tethers don't replace old ones—they add stabilization. Love isn't a zero-sum signal. The receiver is capable of multiple resonances, each at different depths and frequencies.

Avoiding attachment avoids grief, but it also avoids depth. Without strong tethers, the receiver remains unanchored, anxiety increases, meaning thins, and life becomes smaller. The pain of loss is real, but so is the cost of never bonding.

Every bond ends in distance—through change, separation, or death. Knowing this doesn't cheapen love; it sharpens it.

Impermanence encourages presence, attention strengthens resonance, and care becomes deliberate. The receiver doesn't cling—it attunes.

Love and grief expose the deepest truth of the receiver model. We're not isolated minds. We're coupled systems, shaped by resonance. Consciousness isn't something we possess—it's something we share. Which brings us to the final boundary: If consciousness is accessed rather than produced, what happens when access ends entirely? To explore that edge, we must go out of range.

CHAPTER 9
OUT OF RANGE (DEATH & NEAR-DEATH EXPERIENCE)

Let's face it: death is the one topic none of us can avoid, but most of us would rather not talk about. We tiptoe around it with euphemisms—"passed away," "gone to a better place"—as if softer language could soften the reality. Science, for its part, tends to be brisk and clinical: when the brain stops working, consciousness ends. Simple, right? But the truth is, the data doesn't always cooperate with that tidy story.

The Near-Death Experience: A Universal Pattern

Across cultures and eras, people have reported near-death experiences (NDEs) that are strikingly similar. These aren't just stories from the deeply religious or the highly suggestible. They come from people of all backgrounds, including skeptics and clinicians. The details vary, but the core elements repeat: a sense of leaving the body, heightened clarity, panoramic memory, encounters with light or presences, overwhelming calm, and a reluctance to return. These experiences often happen when the brain should be failing—during cardiac arrest, trauma, or anesthesia.

What's truly puzzling is that NDEs are often described as more real than ordinary life. People report vivid memory, expanded perception, and a sense of unity or peace. According to the standard model, the brain under extreme stress should produce confusion and fragmentation, not clarity and coherence. But that's not what people describe. Under the receiver model, this makes sense. As the body shuts down, the filter collapses, resistance drops, and the "antenna" clears. The signal comes through in a way it never could during ordinary life.

Ego Dissolution and the Life Review

Another common feature is ego dissolution. People lose their sense of "me," but instead of feeling annihilated, they feel included—part of something larger. Fear and urgency fall away. The firewall disengages. The receiver stops filtering experience through the survival narrative. What's left is relief, not terror.

Many NDEs include a panoramic life review—an instant replay of one's life, often from multiple perspectives. People describe not just seeing their actions, but feeling their emotional impact on others. If memory is just stored in the brain, this shouldn't be possible, especially when the brain is compromised. But if memory is access, not storage, and the filter is gone, then everything could be available at once.

Perhaps the most controversial part of NDEs is their emotional tone. Even people with no spiritual beliefs report feelings of unconditional acceptance and connection. The receiver model offers a simple explanation: fear is a function of separation. When the filter dissolves, so does separation. The experience of unity isn't imposed—it's revealed.

The Shadow Side: Distressing NDEs

Not all NDEs are peaceful. Some are distressing, filled with fear or confusion. These cases matter, too. Under the receiver model, distress arises when the filter collapses unevenly—ego dissolves, but threat processing remains. Access without preparation isn't always blissful.

Scientific Explanations and Their Limits

Skeptics have plenty of explanations: oxygen deprivation, neurotransmitter surges, temporal lobe disruption, cultural priming. These factors probably play a role. But what they don't explain is the structure and consistency of NDEs across cultures and belief systems. Hallucinations from fever or drugs are usually chaotic and fragmented. NDEs are often coherent and transformative. The receiver model doesn't deny the brain's role—it just suggests that disruption doesn't always mean fabrication.

One of the toughest challenges for the "brain as generator" model is that some NDEs happen when measurable brain activity is minimal or absent. This doesn't prove consciousness exists independently, but it complicates the idea that less brain activity always means less experience. Sometimes, less activity seems to coincide with more.

Another puzzle: how do people form vivid memories of NDEs when the brain is supposedly offline? If memory is about access, not storage, then maybe recall doesn't require intact encoding machinery at the time. Again, this doesn't prove the receiver model, but it makes the phenomenon less paradoxical.

Cultural differences shape the imagery of NDEs, but the core structure—separation from the body, altered time, life review, emotional clarity—remains remarkably consistent. Culture shapes interpretation, but doesn't fully determine experience.

Living in the Face of Death

So what does all this mean for how we live? The receiver model doesn't claim to know what happens after death. It simply suggests that consciousness may be larger than our access to it, and that the end of access isn't necessarily the end of existence. Living well, then, isn't about maximizing output or securing a legacy. It's about tuning your attention, nurturing relationships, and caring for the quality of your experience while you're "in range".

Grief, in this light, isn't just about loss. It's about adapting to distance. The bond mattered because it was real. Its persistence, even in altered form, is what makes grief survivable. Understanding death as disconnection, not erasure, doesn't eliminate grief—it deepens it, but also grounds it.

Humility at the Edge

In the end, the receiver model doesn't solve death. It offers a frame that accommodates the data without flattening experience or inflating belief. It lets us stand at the edge, not with answers, but with orientation—and maybe, with a little more humility and wonder.

CHAPTER 10
THE RETURN (LIVING AS A RECEIVER)

Every way of thinking about consciousness comes with its own built-in advice for how to live. If you see the mind as a machine, you'll focus on optimization. If you see it as a story, you'll chase coherence. If you see it as an illusion, you'll aim for detachment. But if you see the mind as a receiver, the ethic is different. It's not about transcendence or escape—it's about tuning.

Here's the good news: you don't have to "believe" in the receiver model to benefit from it. Think of it as a tool. You don't have to reject neuroscience or embrace mysticism. You don't have to be certain about death or meaning. The receiver model is just a frame—one that might help your experience make more sense. If it clarifies your life, keep it. If not, let it go. Nothing essential is lost.

So, what's the most practical takeaway? Attention is how you tune. What you focus on gets stronger. What you repeatedly expose yourself to becomes your background signal. What you ignore loses power—not because of morality, but because of mechanics. This reframes self-control: you can't will yourself into clarity if you're constantly bathing your nervous system in threat, outrage, and distraction. No amount of discipline can compensate for constant interference. Living as a receiver means treating your attention as precious infrastructure, not disposable fuel.

Most self-improvement advice targets behavior, but environment is often more decisive than willpower. Silence restores bandwidth. Rhythm stabilizes regulation. Predictability lowers resistance. Connection buffers noise. This isn't just lifestyle advice—it's systems maintenance.

Selective ignorance is a skill. Not everything deserves access to your nervous system. Not every issue requires your emotional participation. Not every stimulus improves your understanding. Wisdom isn't about removing the filter, but about adjusting it consciously.

Relationships become regulators. You start to notice not just who shares your values, but who stabilizes your system. Who clarifies you, who drains you, who expands your capacity, and who injects noise. This isn't about moral judgment—it's physics. Love deepens tuning. Chronic instability degrades it. No amount of good intention can override sustained interference. Choosing relationships becomes an act of regulation, not just obligation.

Meaningful work isn't just about passion or productivity. It's about coherence. Some people burn out in prestigious roles, while others thrive in modest ones. The difference isn't talent or effort—it's alignment. When your work resonates with your internal signal, energy circulates. When it doesn't, resistance builds and fatigue follows. Endurance isn't the same as purpose.

Perhaps the most humane implication of the receiver model is what it removes: shame. Anxiety becomes overload, not weakness. Depression becomes disconnection, not failure. Psychological struggle becomes a tuning problem, not a character flaw. Responsibility remains, but cruelty does not. Treatment becomes regulation, not repair. Progress becomes range—the ability to feel, respond, and recover—not just happiness.

For those drawn to spirituality but wary of dogma, the receiver model offers something rare: reverence without certainty. You don't need to believe in immortality to live as though attention matters. You don't need metaphysics to practice presence. The sacred becomes functional.

Ethics, in this frame, aren't commandments—they're consequences. Cruelty distorts signal. Deception injects noise. Kindness stabilizes networks. Attention heals. Not because the universe is watching, but because systems are coupled. You live inside what you amplify.

Living as a receiver doesn't require dramatic change. It's about ordinary practices, taken seriously:

- Silence without distraction
- Sleep without apology
- Movement without optimization
- Conversation without performance
- Grief without timetable
- Attention without fragmentation

None of these are glamorous. All are effective.

You will mistune. You will overload. You will numb out. You will chase noise. This isn't failure—it's the cost of being embodied. Retuning is the practice.

If the brain is a receiver, you're not a closed system struggling alone in an indifferent universe. You're a node in a vast field of experience, temporarily localized, partially filtered, and profoundly connected. Your task isn't to escape the human condition—it's to inhabit it well. To tune without clinging. To connect without collapsing. To filter without numbing. To listen without drowning.

This book doesn't end with answers—it ends with orientation. If nothing else remains, let this remain: You are not broken. You are not isolated. You are not required to know more than you can. You are a receiver. Learning how to live as one isn't a destination. It's a practice.

At the edge of certainty, you stand as a receiver, briefly in range. What you attend to matters. Who you attune to matters. How you live while the signal is available matters. The rest remains unknown. And that, perhaps, is exactly as it should be.

Summary of the Appendices

APPENDIX A
SCIENTIFIC CONTEXT, BOUNDARIES & CAUTION

This appendix sets out what the receiver model actually claims—and what it doesn't. The model suggests that consciousness isn't fully explained by brain activity alone. Instead, the brain modulates, filters, and regulates consciousness, much like a receiver. Evidence from anesthesia, psychedelics, near-death states, and brain injury shows that reducing certain brain activity can sometimes increase subjective richness, not diminish it. Memory persistence and phenomena like terminal lucidity challenge the idea that memories are simply stored in the brain.

Importantly, the receiver model does **not** claim proof of an afterlife, souls, or that neuroscience is obsolete. It's compatible with modern physics, which already accepts non-locality and fields. The model is offered as a framework for coherence, not as a doctrine or final answer.

APPENDIX B THOUGHT EXPERIMENTS & ANALOGIES

Here, the book uses analogies to clarify the receiver model. For example:

- **The Radio Analogy:** Radios don't generate music—they receive it. Damaging the radio doesn't destroy the broadcast, just the reception. The brain behaves similarly.
- **Crowd Panic:** Emotions can spread instantly through a crowd without explicit communication, showing how networked systems can carry state.
- **Memory as Coordinates:** Memory is like revisiting a point in spacetime, not pulling a file from storage.
- **Trauma Firewall:** Trauma doesn't erase memory; it blocks access. Therapy lowers resistance, allowing reconnection.
- **Near-Death Bandwidth Collapse:** As biological regulation fails, the filter drops and access widens, explaining expanded experience during near-death states.

These analogies aren't proof, but they help make the model's structure more understandable.

APPENDIX C
GLOSSARY OF KEY TERMS

This section defines the core concepts of the receiver model in plain language:

- **Receiver:** A biological system that accesses and regulates consciousness, rather than generating it.
- **Signal:** The non-local information that becomes conscious experience when accessed.
- **Filter:** The brain's mechanism for restricting bandwidth to enable functional identity and action.
- **Bio-Damping:** Biological processes that reduce signal intensity for survival-focused consciousness.
- **Noise:** Anything that degrades clarity—stress, overload, trauma, constant stimulation.
- **Tether:** The resonant bond between receivers, formed through emotional synchronization.
- **Resonance:** Mutual alignment that allows efficient information exchange.
- **Default Mode Network (DMN):** The brain network associated with self-referential processing.
- **High-Gain Receiver:** Someone with heightened sensitivity to emotional or informational signals.
- **Signal Hygiene:** Practices that protect and stabilize access to conscious experience.

APPENDIX D COMMON OBJECTIONS & HONEST ANSWERS

This appendix addresses the most frequent questions and criticisms:

- **Isn't this just dualism?** No, the receiver model isn't classic dualism; it's about roles, not substances.
- **Why not panpsychism?** The receiver model avoids saying all matter is conscious; it focuses on access and regulation.
- **Is this just a metaphor?** It's a model, like any scientific model, and makes testable claims.
- **Could AI be conscious?** Possibly, but not by computation alone—consciousness would require integration, filtering, and regulation.
- **Is this incompatible with atheism?** No, it doesn't require belief in God or souls.
- **Isn't consciousness an illusion?** Even illusions require experience; the model takes experience as data.
- **Does this undermine personal responsibility?** No, it reframes it—people are responsible for seeking regulation and reducing harm.

- **Is this dangerous for mental health?** Only if misunderstood; the model emphasizes containment and regulation, not removing all filters.
- **Why hasn't science proven this?** Because subjective experience is hard to measure; the model offers explanatory leverage, not final proof.
- **So what should I believe?** Nothing you don't need to. If the model helps, use it; if not, discard it.

The appendix closes by emphasizing that the receiver model is a stance, not a conclusion. It encourages uncertainty without despair, skepticism without dismissal, and wonder without dogma.

NOTES & FURTHER READING — SUMMARY

This section is designed to help curious readers explore the intellectual background and influences behind the receiver model. Instead of in-text citations, the book offers a curated list of works that inspired or parallel its ideas. These aren't endorsements or proofs, but starting points for deeper exploration.

Key Themes and Recommended Reading

Consciousness & Philosophy of Mind

William James — The Principles of Psychology

James proposed that the brain may act as a "transmissive" rather than productive organ of consciousness. His work remains foundational for non-reductive accounts of mind.

David Chalmers — The Conscious Mind

Introduced the "hard problem" of consciousness,

articulating why subjective experience resists purely physical explanation.

Thomas Nagel — "What Is It Like to Be a Bat?"

A concise and influential argument demonstrating the limits of objective accounts of subjective experience.

Henri Bergson — Matter and Memory

Anticipated receiver-style interpretations of memory as access rather than storage.

Neuroscience & Brain Function

Michael Gazzaniga — Who's in Charge?

Explores how narrative selfhood emerges from neural processes without fully explaining subjective unity.

Anil Seth — Being You

A grounded exploration of predictive processing that complements—but does not resolve—the receiver model's questions.

Stanislav Grof — The Holotropic Mind

Documents non-ordinary states of consciousness encountered in clinical and therapeutic contexts.

Karl Lashley — "In Search of the Engram"

Classic experiments demonstrating that memory does not localise cleanly in brain tissue.

Psychedelics, Filtering & Conscious States

Aldous Huxley — The Doors of Perception

Introduced the "reducing valve" metaphor that remains strikingly relevant.

Robin Carhart-Harris et al. — Psychedelic research papers

Show that decreased Default Mode Network activity correlates with increased subjective richness.

James Fadiman — The Psychedelic Explorer's Guide

Practical observations of altered states without metaphysical overreach.

Memory, Trauma & Identity

Bessel van der Kolk — The Body Keeps the Score

Demonstrates how trauma persists beyond conscious recall, aligning with access-based memory models.

Antonio Damasio — Self Comes to Mind

Explores embodiment and emotion as central to consciousness.

Mental Illness & Psychosis

Eleanor Longden — "The Voices in My Head" (TED Talk)

A first-person account that reframes voice-hearing as experience rather than defect.

R.D. Laing — The Divided Self

A controversial but insightful attempt to understand psychosis from the inside.

Love, Attachment & Grief

John Bowlby — Attachment and Loss

Foundational work on attachment as regulatory system rather than emotional preference.

Colin Murray Parkes — Bereavement

Clinical insights into grief as adaptation rather than pathology.

Near-Death Experience & Death Studies

Raymond Moody — Life After Life

Popularised near-death experience research while raising important questions.

Sam Parnia — Erasing Death

Examines consciousness during cardiac arrest with medical rigor.

Bruce Greyson — After

A cautious and clinical exploration of NDE reports.

Physics, Fields & Information

David Bohm — Wholeness and the Implicate Order

Introduces a field-based understanding of reality that resonates with non-local consciousness models.

Max Tegmark — Our Mathematical Universe

Explores reality as information structure, relevant to non-material interpretations of mind.

Skeptical & Critical Perspectives

Daniel Dennett — Consciousness Explained

A rigorous defence of reductionism that clarifies exactly where it falls short.

Patricia Churchland — Neurophilosophy

An important materialist framework that highlights unresolved explanatory gaps.

A NOTE ON INTERPRETATION

Readers are encouraged to approach these works critically. The receiver model does not require agreement with any single author or theory. It borrows structure, not dogma. No citation in this list constitutes proof. They represent a conversation that remains open.

CLOSING NOTE TO THE READER

Curiosity is not belief. Wonder is not gullibility. Skepticism is not dismissal. The history of understanding is not a march from mystery to certainty, but a slow refinement of better questions. This book offers one such question.

ABOUT THE AUTHOR

J.R. Santana is driven by a lifelong fascination with the mysteries of consciousness, weaving together insights from neuroscience, psychology, and philosophy to illuminate the hidden dimensions of human experience. Santana's work is known for making complex ideas accessible, compassionate, and deeply relevant to everyday life. In addition to a holding a Master's Degree from Cambridge University, Santana is a multi award-winning screenwriter and producer, with two BAFTA nominations. This unique blend of scientific curiosity and storytelling expertise brings a fresh, engaging perspective to Beyond the Brain—an invitation to rethink what it means to be conscious, connected, and fully alive.

www.ingramcontent.com/pod-product-compliance
Lightning Source LLC
LaVergne TN
LVHW050923210926
848482LV00012B/521
* 9 7 8 1 9 1 9 4 6 1 8 1 6 *